The Strange Woman

Revised Edition

Zoë Dee

The Strange Woman

 Scripture quotations marked (KJV) are from The Holy Bible, King James Version. Cambridge Edition: 1769; King James Bible Online, 2016, public domain.

The Strange Woman

Dedication

I dedicate this book to my daughters, both natural and spiritual. May you never find yourself in these circumstances as the strange woman, and may you stay in the path of the virtuous woman. I pray that my experiences and my testimonies will help to influence you in the correct path.

To all the strange women, may this book release you from every strong hold that has held you captive. **The freedom is to die for!** 😊

Acknowledgements

I must acknowledge my Father, my Yahweh – for His grace, for his deliverance, for his everlasting love. He never stopped chasing me and for that, I am grateful.

I must acknowledge my husband, my lord, my “promise” – for continually supporting everything Yahweh has called me to do. Thank you for accepting my past and propelling my future.

I must acknowledge my spiritual leaders, who continued to pray for me and even my spiritual connections who kept me lifted and covered as well.

Strange Woman Chronicles

- Are You the *Strange Woman*?
- To Share or Not to Share?
- "So Pick Me, Love Me, Choose Me!"
- "Vodka/Red Bull"
- "Girl! Don't You Mess with That Man's Wife!"
- The Counterfeit "*Mister*"
- Hot...as in "**Hell**" Hot.
- The Finale
- *The Growth*...Uh Oh

ARE YOU THE STRANGE WOMAN?

Strange:

Why does the scripture use the term "*strange*" in reference to the type of woman that men need to stray away from?

Selah.

In the scriptures, Yahweh speaks of being a stranger in a foreign land, not offering up strange incense, not serving strange gods… and then, the provides detailed instructions and warnings to keep *men* from the *strange* woman. As I meditated on this word "*strange*", I thought about the many times I've heard the phrase, "*What up stranger?!*" from someone who definitely was not a stranger.

After all, what is a person saying when addressing you as "*stranger*"? They are insinuating that they haven't seen or heard from you in a while, that you've been "*acting funny*" in a sense, right?

Strange by definition means unusual, foreign, or even hard to understand. Think of when you find something to be "*strange*" in concept - it is hard to understand, correct? The "*strange*" woman, or we could say - the hard-to-understand woman, the foreign woman, the woman who is not, once again, familiar.

Relating this biblically, in the sense of being a "*strange*" woman, (to me) would obviously mean that there is an expectation of a familiar woman. Does this mean familiar in the sense that the man will know her, as in know her personally? I think not, otherwise the man would have to know basically every single woman on Earth! No, I submit to you that this "*strange*" woman is a woman who is strange in nature spiritually.

It is the strange woman that the Bible gives repeated warnings against being seduced by. It is the strange woman that the Bible says her end is destruction. It is the strange woman of whom the Bible warns that her path has slain many. I think we passively speak on this a lot, sometimes even pridefully. Indeed, a woman has the potential to make or break a man; but do we ever consider this far more beyond what the eye can see?

From the naked eye, we would think that a woman like this is by far the worst of the worst, right? But, really, what if she's not "*strange*" in the sense as we may know "*strange*" to be?

What exactly am I trying to say here? See… we women have believed for far too long that we "fit" the qualifications of being a good woman. For some reason, we have measured ourselves to <u>some</u> standard that has given us the green light to boast and brag on how *good* we are to our men. Most of the time, this bragging comes from women who are single - and continually repeat a cycle of failed relationships; yet time and time - they continue to boast about their worth and how they are better off without their ex-es. The boasting usually comes with the prideful stance; a stance that convinces them to believe that they are ultimately the "it" and they are the ones who deserve better.

"Women like that 'pretty' and they single...and gone be 'pretty single' for a long time."

- Lakendrick Davis

Don't get me wrong, I've had my share of men who definitely had not grown into the maturity of themselves to be the man I needed - **however** - as the years passed, I kept finding myself in the same situations. I finally had to say to myself, ***"Yo, you're literally the only common denominator between you and your ex-es."*** As I prepared for this title, it seemed to me that Yahweh highlighted my "strangeness" more times than not, showing me where I strayed from my teaching - as the strange woman in and of herself has done.

Proverbs 23:26 – 28 KJV

26 My son, give me thine heart, and let thine eyes observe*
my ways. 27 For a whore is a deep ditch; and a strange
woman is a narrow pit. 28 She also lieth in wait as for a prey,
and increaseth the transgressors among men.

Hmm, say what? She "***increaseteh the transgressors among men***."

I find this last little part interesting to note – that she increases the transgressors among men. She creates more transgressors. I mean, again, nothing new because this is the type of power that women brag about. However, I had to see that this was also very applicable to the so-called "*good girl*." You know, the ol' faithful girlfriend; the one that plays the wife without the ring for years and years. She "*takes care of her man*" by taking care of their home, cooking for him, cleaning for him, caring for the children, and sexing him really good because "*that's her man*" and "*that's what she's supposed to do*." Sound familiar? I know you probably can't relate but you just may know someone who can. I'll start with myself. This was me, relationship after relationship.

Oh, I know, you probably thought we were just going to talk about the women who are proud to be the strange woman.

No, we are going to dissect this woman in every shape, form, and fashion. We are going to dive into very clear distinguishments between the woman that expands the life of her king and the woman who brings him down.

You may now be thinking, "*Dang, am I the strange woman?*"

Good, because that's what this book is about. 😊 If you don't know now, you'll definitely able to answer that truthfully at the end of this book.

"If you're not in covenant with the man you're sleeping with, you're a strange woman...you are his whore; you may be a committed whore - but you're his whore."

- Zoë Dee

To Share or Not to Share?

Growing up, you're taught to share, but there were limits. Like, you didn't share "*common sense*" type of things like toothbrushes, or your hair combs and brushes. I learned this early in elementary; I remember, being told to never share brushes in particular because the person could have lice or ringworms or whatever. That makes sense.

I didn't quite get the warning not to share your boyfriend or anyone else's boyfriend but of course, this seemed to be something that was embedded into majority of us; at least I would hope and think so.

For this reason - for the most part - I've always wanted my own "man", one that would be completely committed to me and love only me. This was something I took pride in as a "*good*" girl. Any man (really, boy) that had me knew that I was faithful and if I was with you, I was with you, and you only; you were literally the only one that could mess that up.

I believe maybe even females knew as well, that they could trust me with their boyfriends or men. Hearing all the horrific stories about backstabbing family members sleeping with their friend's/family's husband and all, it was like a thing you just didn't do - a line that you just did not cross if you were really a "*good*" woman.

So, exactly how did I find myself on the other side? The side that says, "*What she don't know won't hurt her?*"

Thinking about it, It's funny or should I say interesting how this situation still has a slight haunt on me. Even though I was too young to even be considering a relationship at that time, it was definitely the first time in my life that I really was the side chick. I was with the D_2 factor (named from my previous title "*#aCall2Purity*") at the time - about fourteen or fifteen, and well… at almost two years, I was pretty much fed up. But not fed up enough to leave, just kind of on that "*If he can do this, I can too.*" I could never quite prove his infidelity but the crabs I'd contracted was kind of… hmm, evident enough, right?

How long was I expected to be faithful? I had to finally worry about myself, right?

Right.

So this guy came along, and truthfully was one of the sexiest young boys ever in school – I'm talking, ooooo just gorgeous! He had eyes for who? Me! But. He had a girlfriend too. Hmm.

Even worse? You probably guessed it. The girlfriend and I weren't "best friends" but we were definitely in the same circle, and we were close enough for me to feel some type of remorse. Like, we were "cool" and probably had "best friend" potential.

I saw this girlfriend and was close to this girlfriend nearly every single day, if not daily. I saw them both together, nearly daily, if not daily! Everyone knew they were a couple as much as they knew about my own relationship. We even went on school trips together and yep, I was the one watching them cute in public in the daytime and screwing him later that evening. I remember even one time being on the phone with the couple together, convincing them to work through their problems! Me. His new side chick. SMH!!!

Honestly, I can't even recall how it all started. She was a good girl too, so I don't even think it was a "what she's not doing" type of thing! It was probably just lust - some flirting, slick messages, I don't know. But sooner or later, there we were - messing around and having sex. We had to have been mad intentional about getting what we wanted because literally, between school and our parent's strictness - I'm sitting here thinking, "*How did we pull that off!?*" I have to shake my head at myself even considering it however, for a short period of time - we did.

D_2 never found out. I don't think I ever confessed either. It was something completely easy to do. That's the thing about being the "*good girl*." You're rarely suspected to betray your boyfriend or really anyone. Though manipulative, I liked my "*little secret*." He was sexy and his sex was waaaaaay better than my boyfriend's. For a window of time - I didn't care about what we were doing, who I could be hurting, or even how I was hurting myself. See, this is the seed of witchcraft – manipulation. Harmless little lies, so we think, and deceit truly weave a tangled web! I shudder to think what would have happened if I had to come face to face with myself in that experience. I could only imagine the hurt that she would have experienced. *See, in my own hurt, I had become someone else.*

I had become the female I hated to deal with. Being cheated on, I knew how it felt. I knew how insecure I was because of this. I knew that I was wrong because, while he was te one that "owed" his girlfriend faithfulness - as a girlfriend, I considered faithfulness a thing to be honored. As a woman, wasn't it a honorable code to not share another woman's personals?!

But see, for too long I'd fought for this characteristic of faithfulness from a partner so it was almost hard to believe that it was attainable. So I thought, in my hurt, "W*hy not simply just play the game I've been dealt?*" This is what everyone apparently does - there was no code of honor when it came to love and lust it seemed.

This was my very first encounter with the seed of being "*the strange woman*." Though young, it wasn't too early to walk in purity - less known walk in integrity of respecting myself and another's relationship. As I look back on that experience, it was something I never wanted to be. Even now, being older, the girlfriend and I are still in somewhat the same circle – and we have been for years. She smiles, hugs me, we have small talk and yes, even now - it hits me seeing her when I think about it; honestly, I still can't see her without thinking, *"Dang, I did that to her."*

When they "*broke up*", I wondered if I was the cause, if she ever knew that he was cheating and that it was me. Maybe I wasn't the only one he was sleeping with however, still decades later - I deal with the reality that I became the very type of woman I hated to deal with.

Yes, I fell into that, "*I don't owe her anything*" excuse but let's be real, it's just an excuse. I was completely wrong - one, to even be having sex in the first place but to disrespect the boundaries of another's relationship was fuel on fire.

What was the guiding force?

Rejection played a part surely. To be rejected by my current boyfriend, was one thing but honestly - I was dealing with much deeper-rooted rejections. On the surface, it was simply the issues with my relationship. However, at the root - this rejection began at a very young age. Let's stay on the surface for right now. So...

I was hurt by previous experiences of being cheated on. I was really feeling insecure and the attention given to me by this other person was everything I really wanted. Can we be seriously transparent here? I didn't really want him. I wanted attention. I wanted validation. I wanted to know that I was *wanted.* This guy, in all in fineness saw me – and wanted me. He was a counterfeit fill to a wounded soul. If you've ever been in this situation or maybe are in it now – ask yourself, what is it that really is pulling you into this situation that you know you shouldn't be in?

Remember, I also had lost hope. I had no faith in an untainted love. I had no faith in a man being one hundred percent faithful to me and only me. So what was the alternative? It was to worry about what pleased me and only me. Not only that was I feeling rejected and then, at this time I was also questioning my sexuality. My girl crush and I, although we were conversing, was older and I don't think that she was feeling me like I was feeling her. Then again, she was confident in who she wanted to be. I wasn't, so now I can see where she stood.

Thinking back on all of this, I'm like, "*Girl you were messed up!"* I had a boyfriend, was sleeping with somebody else's boyfriend, and making moves on a girl - all at the same time. Goodness...GRACE!

Grace kept my heart so that I could ultimately become the woman I was destined to be. Sadly, there are still women who haven't been delivered from this spirit; this spirit of "*I'll have whoever I want, by whatever means necessary.*"

Could it be that the spirit of rejection has had an opportunity to plant and root itself in your heart, dear queen?

But...wait!

Even worse, we blame it on the other woman many times - assuming that the other woman can't be what he needs. Majority of the time we never stop to think about what it is inside of us that needs the attention of someone who is committed to another woman in the first place.

Could it be that we blindly seduce ourselves into believing that we are needed by these "unfulfilled" men, thereby feeling wanted again - i.e. not rejected? Could it be that we are so jealous in nature that we honestly do not like to see other women happy - because we have not experienced that happiness? Could it be that we seriously can only find love in the bed of another because it is this bed that makes us feel accepted?

We are indeed strange women from the very beginning whenever we choose to disgrace ourselves with a taken man, but somehow we justify the immorality in many ways. See, we may not want to admit this - however, there's a nature in us that is manipulative, deceptive, and downright evil.

The truth is, if left to us, we would manifest the very nature of the beast of sin. No matter how tainted a man can be, it is my belief that women can be worse than any man at the game of lies, deceit, and manipulation.

It's in all of us as women and derives from the same source. All of us have the potential to be the strange woman when we aren't yielded to the Yahweh nature in us. It's inevitable if we are not trained. We can tell the best lies, cry the best tears, seduce with the most flattering words - all sourced from the evil one with one purpose: destroy our kings. All, ironically, things that Proverbs warns men of.

I believe this is why the attack within us begins so early; the fight for our purity; the fight for our divinely ordered kingdom. Because we have carry this within us, when we hurt our men – often times, they really don't recover fully. Yes, I know we can justify it by saying, "*They can dish it but they can't take it*," but see this goes hand in hand – our purity and guarding them from the strange woman as well.

When I began studying for the title "*Sexually Wise*", I understood that the woman is the one being on Earth that potentially has the power to destroy a man. This is why the warnings are repeated over and over - to "*DELIVER" thee from the strange woman*!" Once this woman is fully operating in manipulation and deception, it is oftentimes a cycle that is hard to break without intentional deliverance and that is why you have women 45-55 years old playing the same games and more heartbroken than anything – deep down feeling rejected all their lives.

These spirits often manifest with one planted seed - the ugly seed of rejection. Many times this rejection begins with a woman and her father. This was the deeper-rooted issue at hand for me. Abandoned at five by my father – I often felt as if he left me. Later in my teenage years, feeling rejected by my stepfather, embedded in me was the subconscious belief that no man wanted me or even if he did, he would always leave me.

Really take a minute to search yourself through this book. What are your subconscious beliefs when it comes to relationships with men?

The moment a woman feels rejected by a man, subconsciously it is already embedded in her to find that acceptance in a male figure. Sometimes, a woman will go through great lengths for this acceptance. It's like running yourself into a self-fulfilling prophecy repeatedly.

Then there's the fact that women in nature are powerful – we have been gifted and we know this; we are not powerful on their own but because of the ability to channel the spirit realm much more easily. When women tap into demonic spiritual principles, they are powerful in their witchcraft. When they tap into righteous spiritual realms, they are powerful in advancing against the kingdom of darkness. At the end of the day, it's all about who's power we will tap into.

Having that experience at a young age, I could have continued that road. But the Word had already been planted in me enough to desire honesty and integrity. I did not want to be deceptive and manipulative. I say with shame, I can be the best at it; I know because I've torn down a few kings myself in the process of facing my own inner demons. At the end of the day, I did not want to be the woman that I myself hated to deal with. I didn't want to be the cause of another woman's pain. I didn't want to cause the insecurity that I felt

- looking at the next girl like, "*What is it about her? Was I not good enough?"*
While ultimately, I alone couldn't and can't solve the problem of infidelity in entirety, I had to be responsible for the role I choose to play.

This was the reality I had to accept. Eventually, I let all three go. My current boyfriend, my side dude, and my crush. I needed something new. I needed to find myself again and focus on my future, and not based my decisions around a relationship. I needed to honor myself and the principles that I felt in my heart. I'd allowed my hurt, rejection and pain to make me someone that I didn't want to be. I needed to find the root of myself again.

That is exactly what I did the upcoming summer.

I went into my next phase thinking about the type of woman I wanted to be. I often wonder if women ever ask themselves that. You know, *"If I was her, how would I want someone to respect my relationship or marriage?"*

So often we are blinded by our own needs and desires that we rarely think to "do unto others." I was told once that I live by principles that ninety nine percent of the world do not live by and that is a hard pill to swallow. To understand that the one of the biggest misconceptions is thinking that people are raised as you and would treat you (or your belongings) as you would.

Nevertheless, I sought to be single; not rush anything serious. Of course without much guidance - that was short lived and it wasn't long before I found myself again in a "situation."

"Yo, you're literally the only common denominator between you and your ex's."

– Zoë Dee

"SO PICK ME, LOVE ME, CHOOSE ME."

As I think back on several experiences, so many times it boiled down to one person (myself or another) simply wanting to be the "one." How many times do we sing this, see this on our television sets, and even believe that monogamy isn't even natural? While I have different view on multiple wives – there is a difference between a man having multiple wives and a wife or husband being unfaithful.

Having been the adulterous woman and the strange woman in several incidences – it really all manifested from emotions. I wanted to be the center of attention or that person wanted to be the center of attention, if only but for a moment. In #aCall2Purity, I share my first experience as an adulterer. Although I didn't go out of the way to say that I was married in that title, I was.

In the moment of that experience, I would justify my infidelity as "it just happened" but honestly, it did not. It happened because I didn't make a conscious decision to protect my investment and to honor my then husband. As women, we have to take a step back and look at the bigger picture. The thing about this man was that he had been in my life long before I met the man I married and emotional doors were not closed beforehand. In other words, I wasn't fully cleansed of my past. This would play a major role in my marriage as a whole – as my then husband had doors opened as well.

In dealing with the reality of being an adulterous woman or the strange woman, we have to pick through the root – and really dig. We have to ask the hard questions, as I had to the do first time I found myself as a "side chick." We first have to ask – "*Why am I ok with being the secret? Why am I ok with sharing my time with her? Why am I ok with getting leftovers of this person?"*

We also have to ask, "*Why am I ok with giving this person my leftovers?"*

The root of my first experience as an adulterous wife was this exactly. I had unresolved issues of course, but I also did not trust my then husband. Before marriage, we had a very toxic beginning with much drama. A part of me fought for his heart over and over again, all the while never fully releasing my heart to him out of fear.

Yet, I wanted him to pick me! I wanted him to love me! I wanted him to choose me! When he did not (in the sense of committing to faithfulness), it left heavy voids that were easy to come in and fill by others who camouflaged the love, attention, and commitment I wanted. How did I know it was camouflaged? I wasn't given a proposition like, "*Leave him and I'll treat you like you should be treated*." No, this man cried for my love and attention, all while going home to someone else at night as well. But, you see, he "wanted" me. He begged for me. What did that do? It made me feel validated again. It made me feel like I was chosen. It made me feel like I was superior to the next woman because it was me he needed and cried for.

Sigh.

Oh, this heart is so tricky. Do you see the word I keep using? "Feel."

My dear, love is not a feeling – rather a choice. Real love is unconditional and pure. There was no real, substantial love in my adultery, because no real love would have placed me in a situation to say, "*I wanted you; why can't I have you*?"

Do you see how selfish that is? Do you understand how cynical, controlling, and ultimately insane that is? Yet, in my weakest moments – being unfulfilled in a marriage grounded on fickle emotions, it made sense to me. Yes, it made total sense and I placed myself in a situation where I ultimately caused more pain in my budding marriage. To be honest, I likely set the foundation for it.

This is why it's important to have a source of accountability – that is if we want to be free. I don't think that there is any other freedom outside of the blood of the cross. Otherwise, we are left to our own carnality, our flesh – which leads us to death.

I recall, as a strange woman, I sought out someone who was involved with another woman simply so there would be no attachment. What do you know? Attachment occurred anyway. Why? Because – there is a void. The void is there. Hear what I'm saying, many times we seek other men to fill a void but because they are not capable of filling the massive void inside of us – we think another man or woman can.

Now for some people, this void is filled with other things and not people, maybe even habits but the key point here is that there is a void. When we acknowledge this void and we acknowledge the seed that needs to be uprooted, then, and only then – can we be at peace with denying our fleshy desires.

I recall an ex- of mine who contacted me frequently, despite how his current fiancé felt. (This would be the 12 year soul tie ex. I later discuss.) I was so bold to tell this woman that I would not contact her fiancé, but if he contacted me then that was her problem. Why? Because even though she had the ring, and even though they were getting ready to start a family – subconsciously my heart was screaming, "*Pick me! Love me! Choose me*!"

Think about this – why do women fight over men? Why do we have so much drama amongst us when it comes to men? Why is it when we confront a woman or make our argument against a woman, the first thing we bring up is our status and what the man is doing for us and how well he's doing it. Subconsciously we're saying, "*He picked me!*"

We are seeking validation!

We are seeking acceptance!

We need this because underneath everything is a little ugly seed that has been planted in us called, "rejection."

I submit to you that this is the root of every adulterous and strange woman.

Why is it that when we know our man has been with another woman, it makes us feel as if we were not good enough? Because he "picked her," see? He validated her! He loved her! He chose her!

My Lord.

Then what happens? If we fall into the selfishness of filling that void, we fall into the belief that we can have whomever we want and so what if he's taken, right?

So what if he's married and has a family? You don't owe them anything. Something about being able to have that man's attention and affection (regardless of the fact that he's taken) fulfills a part of you that needs to be filled.

What is that doing for you? It's validating you. It's a false void filler because it doesn't last long; when it hits the fan, then you find another one and another one. Your morality declines because you think," What's *the point of having any when it's every man and woman for themselves?"*

You want to be picked.

Let me ask you – can you remember the first time you ever felt rejected?

Can you remember the first man that rejected you?

This is important, because in going back to this moment – you take yourself back to when the enemy entered into your heart and began to sow the seed of this strange woman in you.

For me, as I stated, it was with my father's death. I was only five, but in my mind for as long as I can remember – I felt like he left my mom and I. I believed that if only he'd been with my mom and me, then he would have been alive still. See, he was married a few years after my birth and contracted AIDS (supposedly through his wife). In my mind, I believed that if he loved me, he would have been with my mom and me and he would not have died.

I dealt with this rejection through trying to be the "good girl," thinking if I was just "good enough," then I could keep a man. However, this failed (miserably, I might add) because subconsciously I had already decided in my mind that any man that loved me would leave me. Though my heart screamed, "*Pick me, love me, choose me*!" – my actions were always in defense and preparing for the day when whoever said that they loved me would leave me.

I believe this was an important thing to note when it came to my relationships with men.

I believe that if you'll give the Holy Spirit time to show you, you too will see the root of your rejection and begin your healing. Really, can I tell you a secret?

You have been picked. ☺

You are loved. ☺

You are chosen. ☺

"Good girls often get wifed, but don't get treated right."

– Zoë Dee

"VODKA/RED BULL"

I will take you back with me to Greenville, MS... back a few years in the month of March. I had decided that I needed a break from my home life – having been two months postpartum and needless to say, things just weren't right. My heart was hurt and cold; rebellion was breeding. Spiritually, I was weak. I was pouring into so many others and had released my first title sharing my testimony. My most sensitive area was marriage – and I had just created this group #PrayingWives as a community for building strength in women spiritually for marriage.

But personally? I was tired. I was really beyond tired. I wanted a "*Girl's Night*" which, let's be honest, usually means that we're about to get drunk, talk about our men, and then go home to them (or someone else) for *hopefully* good sex.

This night, I was secure in the fact that I was going to get at least one drink in, shake my poorly off rhythm tail, and go home *as late* as I wanted to for some "*get back*." Even though, in my heart, I really wasn't going out with the intention of cheating; I just knew I wanted to make him feel as insecure as he'd made me feel. That little game we play, you know? Can y'all say red flag? This was definitely not the healthy way to address that situation and even more so, it was not the way to address it as a believer. We must be the ones setting the example in marriages but I'll get back to that.

So, there I was at the bar - rocking to the music (definitely off rhythm, lol) and taking my mind off all of the responsibilities of my daily life. I walked up to the bar, "*Vodka, red bull.*" The bartender asked, "*Single or Double?*"

"*Single*," I replied - no need to go all out, right? A few dances, sweating and flirting later I was back at the bar. Another vodka/red bull. I was in the zone with no care. By this time, far as I cared, I was single and childless. Heck, I wasn't even a professional – do you hear me? I more the drinks kicked in, the less I cared. That night, I just wanted to be free. Here's the thing though that really tugged at me: all night a certain ex- of mine was *constantly* on my mind. I don't know why - I couldn't explain it. It had been **years** since we had talked. He was married (to the woman he'd cheated on me with) and of course, I needed to respect that, right? I pushed him out of my mind the entire night. I refused to even make an attempt to contact him - though again, it had been years since we left off on bad terms - for the second or third time.

Well, while I'm grooving, smiling and free - suddenly I caught a glance of this ex's physical features. Do you know that feeling when your heart drops to your stomach? Like, you literally feel a rush of heat through your stomach?

Yeah...that's what I felt in that moment. I cursed and laughed at the same time. It literally was the last thing that I knew I needed. Of all the people and of all of the nights, why in the heck would he be there in *that* club??? The irony also - neither one of us were people that like to be "out" you know? He was so not the clubber and neither was I. So yeah...It was a divine set up, right? Had to be! Divinely from hell maybe, ha.

"*God, you have a sense of humor*!" I remember thinking.

See, this was a man I would have probably killed **and** died for so *of course,* I could spot him probably ten miles away without glasses! I tried to hide and I avoided him for as long as I could, as I figure out if I would make my presence known to him or not. But it's Specs (Spectators), and though the club had two sides, there were not many places to run. But I can be honest - I wanted him to see me.

Remember, I was feeling some kind of way already. That rejection was heavy. I felt like him seeing me would do something, though I'm not sure what. I wanted his attention. Yet, at the same time, I hated him and seeing him reminded me that I was supposed to hate him **but**, in that moment**,** I loved him. I was two drinks in and realized that this man had been on my mind all night, and it was apparent why. By some force of nature, we were there in spirit before we saw each other in the natural. Something in my subconscious was telling me all that night that we would meet. But why?

I had to go find my friend who I'd come with, who now had the honor of being my designated driver! LOL

****I'll respectfully change the names here, which will also be the names of the upcoming fiction "*Circumcise My Heart.*"**

"*Jacob is here*!" I yelled over the music.
"*WHAT*?!" she asked.
"*Jacob IS HERE*!!!" I yelled louder.

Understanding what I said, her eyes bucked open. I recall her asking me what I wanted to do - if I wanted to leave or stay because she understood that he was probably the last person I needed to see. But I didn't want to leave. He couldn't possibly have that much power over me, right?

Fast forward to minutes later and we finally greet. I shake my head as he hugs me, thinking "*This is not happening*." It was as if the years and distance never existed and we were simple "**Anikka & Jacob**." All of a sudden, I remembered that I was taken again, I was a *wife*. All of sudden, I remembered I was a *mother*, I had children. I was a leader to other women on *fidelity and purity*. <u>But I remembered our memories</u>, familiar spirit again.

I remembered us. Immediately, I was torn between being who I knew that Yahweh wanted me to be and the person I simply wanted to be in **that** moment. And in that moment...I ran to alcohol, not my Father.

"*You gotta buy me a drink*," I yelled to him over the music. He laughed. A laughed that made my insides jump, you know – my deep insides. A laughed that reminded me of the history we shared and the laughter we shared. I rolled my eyes. I ***definitely*** needed another drink.

I thought, "*This could not be my life right now.*"

"*What you drinking*?" he asked.

"*Vodka/Red bull*," I shouted. He looked for a few seconds and I gave him my, "*Don't ask me no questions*," look. "*DOUBLE*." I added.

"*Vodka/Red Bull double*," he ordered. We sat there at the bar together, once again, like old times – engulfed in each other, and no one else mattered. I didn't care who saw us - we started talking like we'd just seen each other the day before. This made matters worse because the internal conflict was becoming heavier. I really should have left because I didn't have any business being there anyway.

So what did I do? I drunk faster! Why??? Why did I even feel like I needed a double on top of the previous drinks? I was already drinking to escape the life I didn't want to go back to and now here I was trying to escape the possibilities of this night. I drunk and drunk fast but I wouldn't let him out of my sight. I started to feel like maybe, just maybe we were supposed to be there together; it had to be, right? The "As We Lay" moment was becoming realer in my mind.

All was well; we laughed, we talked, we flirted...and then I remembered. I remembered the rejection. I remembered he left me and built a family with another woman; not just any woman. A woman he assured me was never anyone for me to be insecure about. A woman he lied to me about, or as he likely would explain – maybe I didn't ask the right questions to get the right answers regarding their relationship. A woman I was insecure about for year. Yes, this was the woman who now had his last name and had borne him children.

I remembered the pain, the nights crying, the ignored phone calls. And all of a sudden, I was walking out of the club - drunk and fighting him, yelling "*You married her! You went and had a family with her! You didn't want me!*" Through drunken sobs and tears running down my face, I yelled, "*WHY WAS I NOT GOOD ENOUGH!*" Things took a complete turn. I could barely walk and as I was being put in the car, I kept trying to get out of the car to get answers from him! Ironically, I still didn't want to let him go and I didn't care anything about who I was obligated to go home to! I didn't care if he had anyone to go home to. I needed him even if I hated him. WHY???

Fast forward a few minutes and he and my designated driver are trying to figure out how I'm getting home. At this point, I make it plain that I didn't want her to take me home. My drunken nature was bold and I forcefully told them that I NEEDED <u>him</u> to take me home. It was well after club hours and I didn't care about a "curfew" from my husband at the time. Crazy...I needed to feel wanted by someone who for years showed me I wasn't his choice. Why?

Is this not the pain that we put ourselves through? Ok, maybe it's just me. Anyway…

They decided that my driver would bring my vehicle home and then he would trail her, with me in the car with him, and then he would take my driver back to her vehicle. It was all fine with me. On the way home, I repeatedly begged him to take me home with him. It was a sad reality, as I cried over and over, "*I wanna go home with you!*" and yet again he was rejecting me. This time, his rejection was for my safety more than not. He refused to take me with him - instead, he took me home and we exchanged numbers. I don't recall the entire conversation but I remember asking him why he was bringing me home; his reply, "*I don't want you like this.*"

It made me love and hate him all over again. I thought, "*Maybe things were different,*" and "*Maybe he realized after all those years I should have built his family.*" This all sounded good - except ... I was a wife, not a girlfriend and he was a husband and neither of us belonged to each other. We were parents. We had careers. It had been years and the decisions we made years ago had drastically navigated us in different directions.

Leaving him, I saved his number under a female friend's name and for the entire next day, it taunted me whether I would delete his number or play this game of infidelity until we were together again as one. I debated long and hard. Hours. I would write messages to him and delete them. I didn't want to be the same person I judged. I didn't want to be an adulterer again. I couldn't imagine living life hiding behind my sins. I had to make a hardcore decision. Why? Because I **wanted what was wrong!** And I was real enough with myself to accept that somewhere along the lines, that I had lost the love for God, my husband, and overall the life that I was living. The question was - was I willing to lay everything down for the feeling of acceptance and love, even if it was false? Realistically, did this man actually love me? Most importantly - even if he wanted me, DID I REALLY WANT HIM? Or did I just want to FEEL loved and accepted?

Another thing I questioned Yahweh on was why did I have the subconscious experience that he would be there or I would see him? In the natural, emotional world it would seem as if we were simply "supposed" to be there. And maybe the "stars aligned" us, hmm.... NO. I had to recognize that underneath all of my other feelings of resentment, rejection, and rebellion towards my then-husband were deeply rooted feelings I had oppressed. In that, that night, I allowed the familiar spirit of my ex- to take root back into my life. See, *I didn't* make the decision to not commit adultery that night - he ex did, because every familiar thing in me wanted him. Though we hadn't been together for years, our sexual ties in the spirit realm were still alive. That is what this night exposed. Now, I praise YAHWEH for keeping us both but it doesn't negate the fact that in the spirit – I was still connected to this man! *In that night, I realized that my heart had become adulterous.*

See this title, "Vodka/Red Bull" is symbolic in two ways. One the natural realm of my experience but also, the psychological aspect of the nature of the drink itself. Why? Vodka/Red Bull is a dangerous one and has the same effect as cocaine (do your own research on that, I need to make other points, lol). I don't know how much my 5'0 body held but listen, I was MESSED UP! So listen, this may not be popular and it may bring strong convictions but let's just take a minute to be real.

Let's take a look at the heart of this issue this night…

1. I left the house with rebellion in my heart against my then-husband, **which let's be honest** - was an open door for my heart and spirit to invite ungodly influence. In hindsight, I should have chosen my home - in any kind of way. I was looking for a "break" but really, I was looking to make him jealous and insecure remember? Look at my heart from the beginning. If I really just needed a break, why chose a "club"? Why not say, "*Hey girl let's go get a bite to eat and a few drinks?"* Why choose to go out with the intention of staying out because I knew that it would piss my partner off? I operated in the spirit of witchcraft because my intention was to do what? Manipulate HIS emotions! Can we be real enough to just deal with us?? Can we face ourselves in all of the ugly traits we may operate in? If not, we tie Yahweh's hand over us and I'll explain that in a bit.

2. This brings me to my next point. I went to a place in which I believe the enemy is given permission to attack our spirits and lure us into ungodly actions - a club. This environment is mainly filled with single people who are drunk (or drinking), women are dressed provocatively, and the music playing mainly influences you to be "loose." Let's be real. Let's cut out the "*it's clean fun*" deception and really ask ourselves if these types of environments grow us as believers? You may say, we must live life and I agree with living LIFE but AGAIN, we're being honest: What in that environment brings you

"life"? It's a temporary high. Is it really what you need? Is it really what you WANT to be doing? Or is it the last result? Is it a habit you don't want to break? Is it just something to do where you can be seen with your fresh outfits, nails, hair, and shoes? Questions that really need answers, you know?

3. Now, this part. My ex. Thinking back, man that was a horrible night, lol. Dang. I seriously just texted my friend while writing this and THANKED HER! **I was a mess**. Seeing that ex under the influence exposed unresolved issues that I was still holding on to. I still loved him, I still felt rejected. I still questioned if I made the right marital choices. I was simply not healed. I should have been *no one's wife.* And this is something men and women do not address. We "heal ourselves" temporarily with new relationships and/or substances. But we don't heal through the power of the Holy Spirit because we usually don't allow Him to have control in this area! We don't forgive. And really what we do is link up with more familiar spirits; people unhealed and rejected as well, and then we bond with them. We don't build emotionally healthy relationships and it stunts the next relationship. So many women are wishing that they were married to another woman's husband. I was one of those women. I have dealt with those women. I can't be the judge of anyone because I've played both roles – and

both are that of *the strange woman.* I know women who still think and feel like I felt that night at Specs. I know this is real. But how can you ever move forward being a victim of the past? How can you have a prominent relationship that works when you're seriously hurting from your past?

See...SO many of us walk about masking ourselves with the "red bull/vodka" combo. You use the strongest combination you can handle at the time, until it's not strong enough and you need something else. Remember, I had two drinks before he came and then increased my "dosage" after he got there. Your combo may be shopping, sex, self-harm, your friends, your family, your children...I mean we use anything really to become co-dependent on whenever we don't want to face the truth. What is this truth?

Well for starters, the truth is that we need to evaluate our decisions and the heart behind them. We are comfortable in the "*God knows my heart*," excuse and yeah, He does; INDEED He does. He knows that it's wicked. He tells us to be led by the Spirit and not the flesh. He tells you that He will lead and guide you into all truth. See...

Let's assume the hand of God wasn't over my destiny that night and that I actually went home with this ex - opening myself up to his demons again through our sexual perversion. I likely would have destroyed two marriages, and

Lord forbid a child or STD could have come; not to mention the sexually transmitted demons as well? I could easily say, "*God knew what I was going through,*" and justify my actions. But here's the thing - I was WRONG. I was wrong to leave the house in that condition of my heart. I was wrong to seek alcohol and become FILTHY DRUNK to mask my hurting heart. I was WRONG to commit adultery in my heart. I was wrong. That situation could have played out so much worse.

But how many times does it play out JUST the opposite and we generally feel no remorse? We become the side chicks ruled by our evil hearts, justifying our actions in our selfishness. People, there's no excuse. Purity is purity, and I'm not just talking about sexual sin but in our lifestyles and everything that pertains to us. God has expectations of our lifestyles and we have no excuse. How many times do we really hold ourselves accountable to righteousness? Now you may not deal with my tests, but I'm sure you have tests! And I'm sure every day you have to choose which voice you'll listen to. You'll have to choose the type of man or woman you want to be based on what's presented to you. You'll have to face the ugly truth of your heart and then compare that with what the Word gives you.

Can I be honest? I cried deleting his number. I was angry

with God. I felt like I didn't deserve what I was experiencing in my current marriage. I felt like I didn't even ask for the life I was given. I felt betrayed by a Father who claimed to love me! Internally, I was tormented with so much! Why couldn't I just go back and sleep with him for even a night!? But... At the end of the day, I needed to take spiritual responsibility for my life and physical responsibility.

How was my adultery going to substitute for my hurt? I deleted the number and didn't look back. Now unfortunately, I was tested again with this same ex- not even too long after that - with almost the exact same scenario. It as if he was placed on demonic assignment to continually pull me back. Nope, I didn't pass the test. I didn't make the right decisions. Matter of fact, when the test came the next time – because I didn't go home with him the previous time, I made sure this time I would get mine! He seemed to appear, again, out of the blue – and that was all it took. At this point, I was on the brink of a divorce. I had no respect or care. The strange woman? I was hell!

The rebellion was even heavier in my heart and I KNEW I was going to do my thing. The common denominator in both of these situations is that I made the decisions with my head and heart but never dealt with the root of the issues that kept me in that cycle. Does that sound familiar? Or is it just me? Ok... And you have to know...I paid for that. Heavily. (I discuss that in the title #aCall2Purity.) The best thing that came out of it the last time was that the chains were finally broken from this man; It took twelve years for this soul tie to be broken! TWELVE YEARS. How much is your disobedience worth?

But anyway, I can't tell you how many times I hear people blame so much of their situations on everything except them, especially *women*. We justify everything that we do, right or wrong! We are a generation, it seems, that cannot be held accountable for anything! But in life? ***Life is based on the decision you make and the consequences of those decisions!*** It's important that we place ourselves on the altar of Yahweh DAILY, all day! *It's important that we submit ourselves to be led by HIM.* It's important that we recognize the weaknesses because guess what? The enemy will take your very weakness to bring you down. Ultimately, this is what happens to everyone. It's the weaknesses we don't want to face and stand up to. We don't wanna admit, "*I'm addicted to sex*", "*I'm addicted to drinking*", "*I'm addicted to masturbation*", "*I'm addicted to playing the victim*", etc. OR even worse, if we do admit it, we have given those demonic influences a right to reside with us and we don't want to change. But we have to do it! We MUST. If we want to see the changes we need to see in ourselves and walk in the calling upon our lives - we MUST allow the water of the Word of wash us, to purify us; we must allow the fire of Yahweh to really (and I mean, REALLY) burn us. Our Father isn't withholding His best from you; it's being stolen by your enemy because of your willing disobedience and/or ignorance to the impact of consequences of your life choices.

OWN THAT. You can have so much better but it's a fight. **Spirit and flesh.** Your flesh will justify and deceive you! Your SPIRIT will convict and heal you! Many of us are missing the BEST life Yahweh has for us because we refuse to humble ourselves to His will for our lives. We also suffer from not realizing that "sin" brings "death." It did before, and it still does! So while it seems we are just "living life" we are really "living dead!" Get that? Because the flesh profits NOTHING! My way out that night was my friend asking me if I wanted to leave. Y'all I will admit, I can be stubborn to a degree. I mean that works when I'm working for the Kingdom or Yahweh but not so much on the opposing side, lol, but now as I see myself and recall this memory: them holding my drunken body up to walk across the street while I sob and scream at this man through tears for leaving me YEARS ago – I am so embarrassed! I mean...There I was married, with kids, and a career and STILL NOT healed from a wound and soul tie probably a DECADE old. Embarrassing? YES! But...

Let me tell you, I'm not the only one. I see men and women everyday carrying hurt and masking it behind sex, self-harm, pills, clubbing, promiscuity, smoking, and more. **These are all roots to the actions and lifestyle of a strange woman.** Can I just leave with the encouragement from this testimony that YAHWEH IS EVERY.THING that you are missing! He will HEAL you. He will DELIVER you. He will allow you to forgive. He gives you a new countenance! He will undo EVERY influence the enemy has taken root in your life. OMG. My vodka/red bulls are long gone because I went through the pain of heart circumcision over these last few years- allowing Yahweh to cut off every piece that didn't reflect Him! Let me tell you, there is so much freedom in dying to live! :)

"Yes, He knows your heart; let Him circumcise it. Let Him get the bad parts out!"

– Zoë Dee

"Girl! Don't Mess With That Man's Wife!"

Woah… now I had my share of being an adulteress woman but that was with men. I have to admit by the time this experience occurred, I had been the strange woman in more cases than not. During this period of my life, I was going through an extreme whore phase. I won't detail it too much here, because I've already written about it but – during this time of my life, I ws really lost. Freshly divorced, broken from a twelve-year soul tie, and regretting every "good girl" decision I had ever made – I had decided it was party time. There would be no "one" particular person. I would do what I wanted, with who I wanted, at any time I wanted. The goal of the game was simply not to become emotionally involved. For me, it should have been easy.

So, it was this guy, and then this guy… and even an ex-sexual partner that had a girlfriend (of whom I contracted an STD from) – and I still didn't care. Before I was off antibiotics good, I was sleeping with another guy. Then there was the girl thing. I had boldly started to accept I liked women sexually and that it was also time to explore that a little wider as well. As I accepted this, it seems it gave my "crushes" a green light to let me know how they'd felt about me. Lord, I shudder to think where I would be if left to my own rescue.

I literally, in the present of my current deliverance, forgot about this experience here. It wasn't that I was trying to avoid writing on it, it simply is one of those things that was really … forgotten, literally – is the best word that I can say. However, as I meditated and asked the Holy Spirit what to write. This experience came up.

If not for any reason than to simply show that boundaries are boundaries - so I pray heed is taken. This woman, she was in a familiar phase I recognized. She was questioning her sexuality – she loved sex with men but was really feeling me. I knew it all too well - the spirit of bisexuality. She was crazed over me. She wanted to always be around me. She flirted with me timidly, and I could call on her for anything.

But, nevertheless… she was married.

I was so cold in those months of rebellion. I cared but I didn't care. After all, women seemed to care nothing about my marriage either. But because she was married, I don't know, something wouldn't allow me to fully engage in her. See, the thing that always was in the back of my mind when it came to women was this – I couldn't trust them. Yes, me a woman refused to ever partake in relationship with a woman because I felt I knew the capabilities all too well. So what was it that I wanted? Sex.

Now, it could have been also that she was not the type of woman I was attracted to. I don't know, but I was cold. I sadly remember forcing myself to pretend as if I was engaged in the flirts and etc. She was also very timid in making moves, if you know what I mean. I wasn't. See, I KNOW if left to my sins, I would be probably the worse of the worse female to be involved in for a female.

Anyway, I remember the day vividly in which I got tired of the back and forth with her. After texting, ifs, ands and what nots - I made sure her husband and children weren't home. I visited her and gave her the desires she wanted while "Playas Club" played in the background. As the details resurface writing this book, I wonder what was it about that movie that gripped her. I'm sure though, it was the same thing that would grip any woman struggling with the spirit of bisexuality. For her, it was likely soft porn – a gateway. I have to sigh. ☹

After I was done, I remember...going in the bathroom, brushing my teeth and having this cold feeling inside; not like the shivers, but like the realization that I had just performed oral sex on a married woman - and I didn't care.

The deception is that many women feel like "it's just how I am," but the reality is that it's not. I can recognize now all of the seeds that yielded fruit to the lifestyle that I was living – and much of it simply was that I was not in the Word, in His presence, nor had I given my whole entire will over to the Father. In fact, I put myself in complete opposition now against His will.

I went from being totally, one hundred percent "RESPECT MARRIAGES" to the complete opposite. I had allowed the enemy to completely distort my hope, my faith and my honor of the covenant. This was like pulling me from heaven to hell in the course of a eight months.

What's even worst? She was one of the women I spent time encouraging in marriage because she was a young wife. So my fall was certainly a bad reflection on the power of Yahweh. What led me to leave her alone was really the fact that a small part of me remembered my own rage as a wife. I wondered what would happen if her and her husband discussed it and he knew about me. I would certainly not be willing to have sex with him, although I was lost in the perversion of threesomes as well. I wondered what would come about if she ended up with an STD from him, and then passed it to me. The possible physical consequences began to weigh on me and no matter how it seemed – we literally were committing adultery. I don't care because it was woman to woman or even if she didn't play the same role in engaging me as I had her – it was pure adultery.

I thought about her husband and then myself as a wife. In Mississippi, you can sue for parental alienation. Yes. Listen, I had court papers in my hand ready to pay for and file against my ex-husband's mistress for spousal alienation. I wanted to burn her to the ground. I had emails they had sent back and forth using their work emails and because they were federal employees, they both could have lost their jobs. I'm telling you, if I ever had a chance to see the main mistress - murder was definitely on my mind.

Somehow, I recalled my own anger and scriptures that warned of destruction that came from sleeping with a married person. Now, part of me still struggled because again, I didn't feel like these scriptures held much weight anymore. After all – all the mistresses seemed to be completely unbothered at their role in the destruction of my family. I never received an apology. I even saw the main mistress and the woman smirked at me. So, I'm like *"God and you said what would happen again?"*

Still, grace pulled me away from that situation and it really was more the fact that I didn't know the state of her husband's mind if he found out about us, nor the state of her mind toward me. She was slightly clingy – and I definitely wasn't trying to deal with clingy. I didn't want a fatal attraction situation.

But wait.... plot twist – so her husband was also bisexual.

See, the thing about having sex with people is you transfer the energy of the spirits of that person you're sleeping with. So, you like girls who like girls? Don't be surprised if after a while, the demons invite more of their friends along to tempt you into being the man that likes men. This is a dangerous thing because the number one thing the enemy loves to attack and distort is identity.

I was really entangling myself into a deeper web and I figured I had too much going on within my own life to be dealing with their drama and uncertainty. Yahweh spared us all in that situation. I don't know why, but I'm grateful! So many people don't come out of their mess! I did, and I can write this book to you today as a warning and as a word of exhortation that you can come out!!!

"Honor. Marriage."

– Zoë Dee

THE COUNTERFEIT "MISTER."

So boom, after all my mess - the Father took me and then cleansed me. It was after I had cried out again to be renewed. I was so far gone – one-night stands, giving myself up after a conversation or two, etc. right. I call that my *hoe phase*. I'll get more into that later because we have made that term like a trophy. So anyway, after my hoe phase - I begged for Yahweh to heal me. I BEGGED.

I told Him if He didn't heal me, I knew the colder I got, I wouldn't be ready for my husband. Suddenly, there was a Holy Ghost fire. Not a huge one, but a burning - like, for real, popping sweat beads and all, right? I remember, it was a Sunday at church during worship. I only felt a touch of His presence but it cleansed me.

Afterward, I had no desire for what I was doing. Then entered the counterfeit. Now, the thing about this counterfeit was that we were friends on Instagram. I didn't know him from anyone else, but somehow … scrolling one day - "*something*" pulled me to his page. I stopped. Literally stopped. I stared at him. A little voice said, "*That's your husband.*"

I laughed. Yes. I laughed like Sarah. Why?
He had a feminine look, for one. Two, he was simply not my type from the looks of it but as you would know… what happened next?

He slid into my inbox on Facebook. I don't even remember how we became friends but the next thing I know, we're liking pictures back and forth on Facebook and Instagram. Now, every time I saw him - I got that little tingly feeling inside of my stomach.

I don't recall the first conversation, but you know…

Eventually we meet. We sat and we talked. He told me that I knew what was up. He told me I know I was supposed to be his wife. He, in such a sexy way, commanded me to put my name in front of his last name. It was like the perfect, PERFECT, set up. (Now that I understand the demonic realm even more, that moment was definitely a moment of demonic entry, but anyway…)

It definitely was a set up. There was an unsettling in my stomach - I fought the reality with my fear. I had prayed. He had appeared. But could I be missing something?
Sooner or later, we ended up having sex. Ha! Yes, I prayed for my husband and then this man walked into my life and I slept with him. Let me make another thing clear that makes this a little interesting. Remember my Vegas phase? There was a complete stranger there that told me that my husband would soon come, but to not have sex with him when he did. Interesting, the very next month – Mr. Counterfeit comes along.

Let me clarify another thing. I prayed for a man that loved Yahweh and that was in church.

Wouldn't you know… this man was in church every single day of the week?! Like literally, not only every day of the week but sometimes even several times a day. He even invited me to come out and though I had some interesting moments – traditional quartet and all that it has just doesn't move me. There was another thing though…

Remember that feminine side? I saw a lot of it come out. I questioned the Father a lot. Was I missing something??? I

I confided in my mom that he and I were seeing each other. Her first response was that she thought he was bisexual. I said, "well I was too."

Yeah…That ended that. I started to think about what it really was that was gravitating us more toward one another. Could it have been the kindred spirits of sexual perversion?

But remember, there was still an issue of our sex life regardless. The spirit of the Lord had fallen extremely heavy on me in conviction about us having sex. I sat down with him and told him that if Yahweh had placed us together and we believed that Yahweh was strategically putting us together for purpose - then sex was definitely off the table. Let me tell you, this wasn't easy. This man had good sex. I often joked with my god sister on not having good sex with many ex's so to have one with good sex was literally addictive! It was illegal (because we were not in covenant) too so you already know the pleasures of sin there.

Smh.

Anyway, we were ok – seemingly, because after all, we are both believers who know the Word and know that we should be sexually pure, right? It would seem that way. But then I found myself going through the normal cycle. I would see him all over social media but not answering my texts. You know, "*OH, I want to see you, but "church" lasted longer than you expected.*" Then, he would come over, maybe after days of not seeing one another and he would be on his phone.

Whew. Then. This "Mister" as I called him, had a heart attack. Now of course I can't see him, and even more, he didn't want me at the hospital. Well, that should be a total flag on play, right?! Ha!!! Lol, but even more, it gave me time to really pray and ask, "*Hath God said*?" It seems everyone I mentioned him too knew him and knew he had a hoe'ish background. I didn't care about that and couldn't judge that. Why? I did too.

I had compassion and understanding of that. But I remember praying for him one morning on the way to work. I could literally see the vessels and blood flow in his heart being renewed. The Holy Spirit spoke and said he was giving him a new heart. I thought this to be spiritual and physical. I kept my distance for protection but stayed reverently in prayer. It was not my ideal situation. We barely saw one another and we barely texted. To say we were "dating" was a joke to me but I found serenity in giving my Father full control. There was something about this man that took a hold of me before we were even in company. There had to have been a purpose.

A few months later, we went on our first official date out of the city. I felt like a star on his arms. Of course, he ran into someone he knew - after all his name is widely known through our hometown and surrounding areas. I felt honored to be chosen and laughed a lot at Yahweh. He was so not my type, but I would let the Lord lead because "my type" kept sending me the through brokenness! Lol

But shortly after that date - and I do mean shortly, I received a text from my God-mom and she asked if I still dated my "Mister." I said, "*Yes, what's up.*"

Y'all already probably know where this is going right?

She tells me that he had just posted a picture with another woman on his Facebook. I went to his Facebook; I didn't see it. I asked her to send it to me. Surely, there was "my Mister" and apparently his "Misses." Lol

I wasn't even mad. I was super calm. Ironically, this day I needed him to pick me up and take me to my car. When he did, we had a pretty normal conversation. Like, the old me would have been completely in his face! Lol it was none of that for me this time.

I pulled out my phone and asked him casually about it. Oh my goodness, he played it off so cool. It was "*just a picture*" but one that I couldn't see on his timeline. Hmmm…

Now that you've gotten a little of the juicy details, Lol, let me bring this back home for you.

The Sunday before - the very day before this happened, I was at the altar and the Holy Spirit asked, "*Are you willing to lay your Issac on the altar*?" When the Holy Spirit spoke this, I knew exactly what He was saying. He, my "Mister" was my *Issac*, my promise of *"greater*" after everything I had went through with my former relationships and marriage; more specifically though – my previous marriage.

I accepted the challenge of being a minister's wife and being the *"First Lady"* I needed to be because it caused me to rise up to a new level spiritually. I understood that I had, myself, had ministry in me and I needed to be connected to a man who would cover me spiritually. But I understood that Sunday on the altar as I cried out in uncontrollable tears - that I needed to be able to surrender him, this promise, to

Yahweh. Not only that, at the altar during prayer (I believe this same Sunday), Pastor prophesied to me and denounced familiar spirits. This is an important thing to note that I will drive deeper into but on that day, so much fear overwhelmed me that day on the altar.

I remember going out to eat with my church member that day (who knew him and believed with me for Yahweh's plan) and telling her about it. I confessed knowing that if I needed to let go - I would just have to.

Now, even more interesting? Two or three weeks prior, I saw in a dream him and in this dream he was on Instagram with another woman. Tell me Yahweh won't warn you and look out for you!!

What happened after that is literally history. The young lady and I ended up talking; wouldn't you know, just in my favor, my God-mom was friends with this woman's cousin! We exchanged our experiences and I let her know how long we had been "*dating*" and etc. Sadly, he had been around her children and of course they were sleeping together - two things we didn't do. I felt more sorry for her than I did for myself honestly.

I was at peace, major peace. It was by far the easiest "break up" ever. Not to say I didn't shed a tear but trust me - it was nothing like I'd ever experienced. Crazy but my Father had me so covered from start to finish. Now, what had to happen was a complete emotional and spiritual disconnect.

I can admit, that because I believed Yahweh, I waited. See, I still had faith that because of my obedience to the Father, things would work out. Until Yahweh told me to let go, I would not. Eventually, he did come back a few months later wanting to "start over." I gave him attention, but of course sex was completely off the table. However, it wasn't long before I realized the ship had sailed, the thrill was gone, lol and I needed healing and a breaking from him. There was a familiar spirit that had attached to me through him and remember – I'd verbally and spiritually connected myself to him. Due to this familiar spirit, he was able to access areas of my heart as the ones before. Remember, I mentioned that I found myself feeling the same; the experience was very familiar. Also, when I spoke my first name and his last name together – I bound us together through my words. I changed my identity by in the spirit and gave him access over me. Then, I consummated that illegal connection through sex. Are you seeing how important this is or all we still going to play?

I had to receive deliverance and healing in my mind. I needed a spiritual breaking to let go completely. It was time to fast! I put myself on a three-week fast but it didn't even take that long!

I remember praying in the Spirit one day reverently so hard. I was crying in the spirit and suddenly I felt a pain hit my stomach. I heard the words, "*LET GO*." I fell over as if someone had punched me in the stomach - still crying and still praying. I prayed until the pain left my stomach.

The peace. The joy. Oh Lord.

I'm just grateful for the journey! You have no idea. After that… I've never been able to look at him the same. We have seen each other and even shared a few messages here and there, but it was literally as if we never had a past.

Oh! Before I forget, he had a little son a few months later. You do the math. Did this make me feel any type of way? No. The son is super cute! When I say, PEACE … I mean PEACE!

The other thing I want to make sure I bring clarity to.

I'm a praying woman. Some of you may be wondering how I missed that, or if I missed it. Well, I will tell you I asked myself and the Father the same thing. Yes, I remember asking the Holy Spirit afterwards why I went through that. After all, I prayed for him to prepare me for my husband, right. His answer, "*You asked me to prepare you for your husband."* Lol, sense of humor, huh but seriously.

I knew that I would be a woman after Yahweh's heart and so would my husband. I found myself in a place where I was willing to sacrifice my desires to have sex for *his* anointing, not even mine! I realized that if I was already called to be his wife, I needed to walk in that faith and obedience and please the Father – not to contaminate the will of Yahweh as I had done before. As a wife, this is what we are expected to do. You don't wait until you have a ring on your finger to get in position. You are a wife before the ring and we have to understand that that comes with a responsibility to walk upright before and after. I don't care how long you've been with a man – how can you be his "good thing" or his "virtuous woman" if we are pulling him into and engaging with him in sexual sin or anything else?

It doesn't work like that when you're in the Father's will. That is the way of the world, not YAHWEH'S. I asked Him to prepare me for my husband and I had to prepare my heart to trust HIM first for that man. Though I knew how to pray, I had to set my heart and faith on praying for this man – believing Yahweh's will above all that it looked like.

I asked Him to prepare me for my husband, and the Mister came along as a part of that purging process. I had to learn how to lay my "Issac" on the altar and believe the Father for a ram in the bush! The hardest but most powerful thing ever was that I had to learn to truly place my heart in the Father's hand. This was extremely difficult for me. I had to believe that if I let him go, regardless, it was working out for ME.

Now, I do believe the spiritual potential could have been there and I saw his breakthrough in the spirit many times through my dreams. I also delivered warnings to him that I believe the Holy Spirit wanted me to deliver. I believe that possibly he was in his own battle – and I was a float for him to grab on to. However, I believe, his free will was evident and Yahweh did not bind me to his rebellion; he saved me from the hurt of that.

I could be wrong.

But I do know that when my husband came along – he wasn't my "type." We had to walk in purity, just as it was required with the counterfeit. There were so many other things that Yahweh dealt with me on during my counterfeit phase that very applicable to the relationship that I built with my now husband.

I don't regret that one, and I don't honestly feel like I "missed it." It worked out flawlessly perfect for me in the end.

More than anything, again, the biggest lesson I learned was that my purity was not simply for me. I could not be the *strange woman* to the future king of my home and then expect Yahweh to bless it.

Are you the type of woman that Yahweh would deliver His son to? Really?

Selah.

"It doesn't matter if you're the "good girl", are you the 'God girl'."

– Zoe Davis

HOT…

AS IN "HELL" HOT

So, at this moment of my life - it's 2016, I've passed and failed a few tests with previous lovers, I will admit. I am also divorced, but healing. I am on a path to purity, again, celibate for months now. My focus is on business and simply waiting for my husband to manifest. But for some reason, I keep being faced with these tests of faithfulness. I will be completely honest…

At this point, I was having a harder decision than ever to respect another woman's marriage - after mine had been disrespected time after time. I mean, if we're living by this whole, "*You reap what you sow*" belief – I did not sow the type of unfaithfulness I received. But what does one have to do with the other though? Why should it matter if other women disrespected my marriage or vice versa? Well, isn't that the justification? *Do what others would do to you*? There's no moral code to abide by in the terms of honoring marriage because *"Obviously his wife ain't doing something right", "Obviously the other woman has something the wife doesn't have*" right? Oh! No, it's "*You don't owe that woman anything – her husband does.*" These are the common excuses for being the mistress. Why then, I wonder, does the Bible specify characteristics of an adulterous woman *and* a strange woman?

Proverbs 5:3-6
3 For the lips of the adulterous woman drip honey, and her speech is smoother than oil;
4 but in the end she is bitter as gall, sharp as a double-edged sword.
5 Her feet go down to death; her steps lead straight to the grave.
6 She gives no thought to the way of life; her paths wander aimlessly, but she does not know it.

Now, this experience is a little different because by now at this point, as I said, I had gone through a few more relationships and two divorces, adultery being a major cause of this as well. (Well, I would actually say that the adultery was a fruit of a much deeper rooter seeds.)

That tore a lot in me, faith wise. One of the worst parts was not only the adultery itself – but had to I come face to face with the reality that one of the women involved not only knew about me as his wife – she knew about my children, my job, and everything. I was blocked from her social media and every avenue to find her – but she knew so much about me!

She was literally waiting for my ex-husband to leave me after I had my child and even more so once she knew that I knew about her and my then husband.

This tore every part of womanhood in me. I think it was easier dealing with the "strange woman" in the nature of sex, but not the "adulterous woman" who was content with falling in love with and disrespecting my covenant so boldly. I can't even begin to explain how this broke me. I think it was because of this, I felt full entitlement to being the option in my next experience. I didn't care that he had someone else – to me it was not about the race for the ring; the race for his attention. Of course, that failed as well but after all of this – just imagine me now in another situation where I have to be considerate of another woman, "because it's right."

So, boom, here I am – after experiencing *all* of this, free from that twelve year soul tie, recently broken up with another man due to unfaithfulness (the counterfeit) sigh ☹, single, minding my business and my children and then…one night.

I went out with a group this night, a group of old high school classmates. It was a chill night, lots of laughs and everything – very cool vibes! Later after I made it home - one of the guys that I was hanging with and I were conversing via text. The interesting part is that until this moment, this man and I had been platonic friends. He'd been like a brother in the sense that he was always "*putting me on game*." He would check me when I was doing too much on social media and literally check in on my mental and emotional wellbeing.

He seemed to have found peace in many areas of his life and I respected him for caring enough for me to ensure I had that same peace. Aside from the that, the man was fine. We had known each other casually since high school but in between his long term relationship and mine, the time for us never aligned.

But this night, grown and married - we fell into what some would say "fate." Yeaaah… *insert eye roll*

For over an hour, we conversed back and forth via texts, contemplating him coming over to spend the night. I wanted him, but not even sexually. Sure, my mind went there of course, I won't lie. I believed the sex would have been amazing but even more than the sex, I just didn't want to feel lonely.

My biggest conflict was that I was now a divorced woman, wanting to spend time with a married man. I wondered if the mistresses from my past ever thought about me and considered me just as I was doing for this woman. I wondered what she believed her husband was doing or where she thought he'd be - while he would have been lying in my bed. Even more, I had been sexually pure for the last few months. Did I want to have to go back to the altar again for having sex with someone else's husband? I knew and understood covenant. But who seriously honored it? This was my problem. Year after year, all I witnessed was unfaithfulness. Was it even a reality?

Strangely, he was so honest that it was luring. He told me he missed his wife, and that he just wanted to hold me. He let me know that I would be, in a sense, basically used for his comfort - just as he would be used for mine. We'd been conversing for a time, so he knew that although I was single – emotionally I was still healing from my ex. This was one of the reasons he invited me out in the first place. It was strange because I'd never had that type of honesty, really. I knew we were attracted to one another but beyond the attraction, we were just two individuals in an extremely unfortunate emotional state. He didn't want me, he wanted the physical presence of me to fill a void – his wife. The (not so funny) thing is, it made me want him to come over even more. It was as if understanding what were doing gave me a false sense of security with him. I can't explain it at all still.

But…I refused him that night with tears on my pillow. I cried myself to sleep; I was angry and lonely. There was no one else to call. I had no other reason to turn him down other than not wanting to disrespect the marriage of a man I highly respected. I had to recall the lessons from "The Counterfeit." He was a great man; I could not put myself in the position to bring him down. I could not be his Delilah.

This hurt. I was beyond angry, I was pissed. I owed his wife nothing. I owed him nothing. I could let him cover over and use his presence just as he would be using mine. But, still, I chose to honor him, his wife, and their covenant. This. WAS. NOT. EASY.

So many times we talk about purity as if it's easy to walk in. It's not. We talk about mistresses in the sense that it should be simple - married men should be off limits. Now, don't get me wrong, yes, they should. But that's only when you're being led by a higher power other than your own flesh. My flesh would have had him in my bed.

My flesh would have justified it because of my own past experiences and in my own carnal thinking, I would have been right. Even if his intentions were just to hold me, there was no way we would not have had sex. We would have had sex and it's possible, we would have continued having sex. The one thing that I understood was that that situation was not what it seemed like it would end up as. It was going to be hell to pay behind this one, after everything that I had gone through before.

I know it because I know that spirit of deception. I had failed myself several times in the past believing that I could get close to fire without burning myself - if you know what I'm saying.

One of the biggest mistakes with women is that we go through these experiences so many times and simply repeat them. We literally, it seems, do not evaluate our choices and the consequences that follow.

Sister and queen, if you keep going through the same things and situations over and over again, as I said – you are the only common denominator. It's not the men – it's you. You are the strange woman. You are the adulterous woman. You need to be free.

"The Holy Ghost will always bring you back home; His love forever chases you."

–Zoë Davis

THE FINALE...

The love of the Father is truly unconditional. After all of the things that I have done – no matter how many times I have dirtied my temple, He has committed to cleansing me.

His loved has literally chased me; I don't know how else to describe it. Honestly, I don't. I don't know how else to explain it either – other than he's loved me like no man ever has! Because I know this love now, I know how to identify it in the natural – and I can say that my husband is a reflection of this love.

I know now also that ultimately you cannot understand the love of the Father and be a strange or adulterous woman. When you have a revelation of His love for you, and His best for you – you find yourself content in Him.

I know this not only through my seasons of falls and rises but the final test – the test of renewing my purity and waiting on Yahweh to align my husband and I together.

The first thing I had to do was place my heart in His hands and trust Him – remember I learned that with the counterfeit! The second thing I had to do was honor my temple. Then, I had to fall into position. I prayed for my husband. I fasted for my husband. I saw him in the spirit realm as my husband long before he was my husband in the natural. I learned to speak life over him as my husband months before we were married. This was essential. I was no longer his strange woman – I was in position now as his wife should be. I covered him – and I prayed over him fervently day in and day out, literally morning and night I was praying as the Holy Spirit led and praying against the enemy's plots over him.

See that? Yahweh cleansed me up, bringing me from a place of being his *strange* woman to his *virtuous* woman. No, I wasn't committing adultery with him – but I was because he wasn't in covenant with me yet, which meant he still belonged to the Father. In having sex with him, I was pulling him out of his destiny. I thought I was a "good girl" but I wasn't a "God girl" for Him.

A good woman, a virtuous woman the Word says, does him good and not evil all of his life! Even the day that he proposed to me, I was "in my feelings" about him (as they say) and the Holy Spirit said to me, "*What are you crying for? Get up and war*!" I heard this three times and finally went into my prayer closet. Hours later, he joined me in the prayer closet and had a breakthrough – and moments later we were engaged.

Had I never experienced "*Mister*" then I would not have been equipped in many ways for my promise. But see, the promise doesn't come without surrender. Yes, I had to surrender my will. I had to surrender doing things as the world does them. I had to surrender and give up casual, committed sex. I was nothing but his committed whore – leading him into transgression. I had to surrender my lust. **I had to surrender.**

But among surrendering, I also had to heal. I had to close every emotional door and cleans from every soul tie. See, my husband came after the season of "Hot…As in Hell Hot" and "The Counterfeit." These experiences were eight (new beginnings) months apart.

What if I wouldn't have let Yahweh lead me with the counterfeit? What if I would have called that married man to my bed that night? What if I wouldn't have fasted and prayed from my breakthrough from "The Counterfeit?" I'll never know and I'm glad that I won't.

I hope that this book has encouraged you in many ways to know that at any moment that you choose, you can let Yahweh in your heart and let him heal and renew. It doesn't matter if you're the strange woman or the adulterous woman, ***are you ready to be the virtuous woman***? ☺

The Growth...Uh OH

(2025 Update)

In 2021, I began to study the topic of biblical marriage as it relates to this title. In doing so, it has that allowed me to understand sexual purity from a completely different angle.

I must end the book with this update to reflect **biblical** accuracy due to my personal conviction, though I understand the controversy that it may stir.

- Since publishing this title, I have learned that *"adultery"* (as defined biblically) is a <u>woman who breaks wedlock and/or a man who sleeps with (or looks upon in lust) a **married** woman.</u>
- I have also learned that the scriptures did not forbid pre-marital sex as a sexual sin (*Leviticus 18*), <u>however</u> – a commandment was given that if a man engaged in premarital sex BEFORE establishing a covenant with a woman (a virgin), then he was required to go before her father to ask for permission to wed her and pay a virgin's price for her. The father could refuse, but he still had to pay. (*Exodus 22: 16-17*)
- I have learned that monogamy was not commanded in the scriptures, and that the first commandment to man was indeed to *"be fruitful and multiply"*; i.e. have sex and have enough of it to make sure you leave seed on this Earth.

- I have learned that the primary biblical marriage structure in the scriptures was and is, in fact, polygyny.
- I have learned that sexual purity for a woman and for a man ***biblically*** are <u>not</u> the same; as only the woman is expected to be with **one** man all of her life.

I understand that these statements are indeed quite controversial and possibly offensive to previous teachings/knowledge. To avoid making this book a lesson on these topics, I ask that you meditate on this title through the lenses given before and after. It may be necessary to seek more understanding/research before continuing the read/study of this title.

Instead of editing the entire book, I thought that by adding this growth I have encountered – it may help to realize why some of the experiences I faced were such within this title. I know for me, the understanding gave me a much better revelation of why I ended up in these situations myself. It is my assessment that many of the issues we find in our modern-day relationships and marriage, are due to forced monogamy, i.e. the western cultural belief that man has to be with only one woman ***biblically***. This was never mandated, and I have resources to show such. However, for the purpose of this book – I'd like to introduce this truth and challenge you to research the topic on your own. Either way, the readings that you will found in this book stand pure – examine yourself to understand if you are *the strange woman* and seek wisdom for how to become the woman with a heart after Yah that you were designed to be.

Blessings,

Zoë Dee

EXCERPT

"CIRCUMCISE MY HEART"

February 15, 2014

I laid there on the old wooden bench crying. The world seemed to be moving. I could hear mothers praying in tongues and wailing in the Spirit. The sounds seemed...I don't know- mute, if I could say. Because all I could hear were the cries of my heart. I did not know if I was crying silently or loudly, but I knew my heart felt as if it was breaking. Each breath of air became harder to breathe in. It felt as if my body was becoming weaker and weaker and, my heart? It was as if I could feel the tears of the ligaments that were holding it in place. I felt death. Nothing but death. I didn't know how to explain to anyone that I was crying this hard over a man…but my heart. My heart was breaking! I wanted to cry aloud for help. I wanted to cry, "*Someone pray for me! I need help! Cover me! Hug me!"* But again...the room, though filled with activity, was mute. I don't remember the songs playing. The once familiar faces were blurry through my swollen eyes. I don't know how long I had been on the floor crying, honestly. I just knew that my heart, *my heart* was tearing. I wanted to tell myself that this was best, that it would soon be ok. That this man would come back and love me; that he would realize that I was a good woman and that me being a Spirit filled woman made me an even better woman! I wanted to believe that soon enough he would realize that all of my prayers for his destiny were for us and well, I just had to persevere. But I couldn't. I couldn't believe this because my mind replayed the images of the constant redails to his phone. And then that one call. Ump. That one call which answered with that familiar voice answering, "Yeellooow?"

My mind froze in that moment. And the tears began all over again as I cried out to God angrily! Why wouldn't He save this man like He'd saved me? Why wouldn't God show him how good of a God that He could be to him, the man that I loved, so that we could just *be together*!? Why was God making me *choose*?! How could a god that loved me so much take away something so precious to my heart away from me?!

Finally, I heard steps coming toward me. A warm hand was on my shoulder. I didn't bother to look up. As much as I wanted the comfort, I still felt foolish! Foolish for laying here crying over a man that obviously did not want me.

"*He's circumcising your heart,*" *Ms. Teresa said, "He says He has to get the bad parts out of your heart.*"

I nodded my head, and my shoulders fell even weaker. I began to cry heavier than before.

I don't know if that was supposed to bring me comfort or if it was supposed to be confirmation. I didn't feel too much of either but those words penetrated a deeper part of me - those words passed my head and passed my heart. Whatever part of me it touched, my heart and mind had to come to subjection to it and soon enough, my tears dried. I didn't quite feel like the abandoned little girl, unheard and unloved. Somehow, I felt a strange peace. Some kind of way, my heart stopped hurting and some kind of way, I knew that everything would be ok.

My mind and heart embraced the words, "*He's bad for your heart*" and beyond what my heart screamed and what my mind tried to justify- I knew *that* day, it was time to let go.

I decided that it was time to embrace the day. My Father had spoken. With puffy eyes and a banging headache, I gathered myself together to listen to the Word. I wasn't ok, but I was ok. It was quite a surreal, numbing feeling. It was as if I was living but living outside of myself. After church, I visited my family for a few minutes and went back home to pack my bags. I was already a few hours behind and had a four-hour drive ahead of me back to campus. As I played a little worship music, and finished packing, "*Are you gonna see Jacob before you leave?*" Mama Bonita asked.

It was her bed I sobbed on the night before and her phone I used to see if he would answer, after numerous attempts from my own number. She didn't say anything thing but, trust me, her eyebrows - rather her eyebrow - said enough.

I hardened my face, "*Mama you know I ain't finna run up behind that boy,*" I lied. I had been running up behind him since we met seems like it. She never liked him, but she never admitted it. I think she knew more than she really ever said, but she always had my back.

"*Ummhmmp baby girl, ok,*" she said.

Almost like clock work, my phone rung, and with his ring tone. I pretended not to see Mama B's facial expression and the folding of her arms. I was almost tickled but I just held my face steady.

"*May I see you before you go*?" Jacob asked.

I had been home a complete forty eight hours and as usual, only twenty minutes, of my time is what he desires. That twenty minutes was probably just to have sex. But either way, I didn't budge. One, I saw Mama watching me but for two, I was numb for some reason. Beyond what my heart and brain could comprehend; yet I was ok.

"*Why?*" I asked.

"*Well, I guess I can show you when you get here*," he retorts.

I rolled my eyes. *sigh*

It would probably be some form of sexual "surprise" which I was over. The more I reflected on the morning at church and what the mother had said, I realized that the dynamics of our relationship had truly changed; I was not the same. I mean, I was but I wasn't. The thrill of late-night smash sessions on dirt roads didn't excite me, nor did getting drunk and going for three and four rounds at a time. Come to think of it, the last time we had sex he was so drunk it was only one round - and a short one at that.

sigh

After thinking of this and the torture I'd been through Saturday night, I finally replied, "*I'll stop by on the way out.*"

"*That's all I get?"* he had the nerve to reply.

"*Apparently that's all you wanted,"* I quickly retorted.

No reply.

Needless to say I was the more aggressive one. Jacob hated conflict and was typically smooth and easy going. That was one of the things I loved about him. He could always calm me down because he reminded me to stay postured. We never argued, unless it was over something stupid, like basketball. Even when we had problems, we discussed them as friends...always coming to some sort of solution. And of course, sealing it with sex. Those were the days I couldn't go a day without him. Now, we may talk every other day and me being four hours away from doesn't help. I wondered how an instantaneous connection such as ours had grown so cold.

About the Author

A product of statutory rape and a byproduct of adultery, Zoë Dee passionately travels statewide sharing her story and teaching young and old how to escape the strongholds and oppression related to premarital sex and adultery by the power of God. She is an educator, entrepreneur, and international known author and artist. Zoë has authored nine titles as including the compelling writings *#aCall2Purity*, *Sexually Wise* and *Sexual Skeletons*.

After nine years of teaching, Zoë left the public classroom to pursue full time entrepreneurship as a speaker, publisher, and life coach. In doing so, she has become a highly respected and desired speaker, as she pours life into every ear that listens. Though no longer in the traditional classroom, she offers her teaching gift to the church, allowing the gift to be manifested teaching young people the Word of God. After an immensely powerful encounter with the Father, she has committed her life to motivate and dare her audience to answer the call to purity. In addition to this – she is a wife, mother, exhortation life coach, and manages multiple family owned businesses.

Current Titles by Author

- **#aCall2Purity**
- **Sexually Wise**
- **Sexual Skeletons**
- **40 Days to Freedom Devotional Journal**
- **#aCall2Purity Course Manual**
- **War Wounds** *(Prayer book for teachers)*
- **Confessions for Wives** *(Prayer book for wives)*

Zoë also blogs at www.zoedeespeaks.com

Upcoming Titles by Author

- **Circumcise My Heart (2021)**
- **#aCall2Purity Couple's Devotional**

Zoë is available for guest speaking engagements as well as her #aCall2Purity keynote message/course.

For more information on booking please contact: booking@zoedeespeaks.com or witnesslegend.com

Connect with Zoë on social platforms on

@ "Zoë Dee Speaks"